Help Me Be Good

Being Rude

Joy Berry
Illustrated by Bartholomew

Joy Berry Books
New York

This book is about Eric and his friends Lennie and Patty.

Reading about Eric and his friends can help you understand and deal with being rude.

You are being rude when you treat other people as if they are not as important as you are.

You are being rude when you insist on being first.

You are being rude when you insist on having the best for yourself.

You are being rude when you insist on having the most for yourself.

You are being rude when you insist that everyone notice you and no one else.

You are being rude when you insist on having your own way all the time.

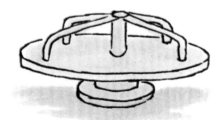

When you are being rude, you are being selfish and unkind.

Other people might not want to be with you when you are being rude.

Try not to be rude. Do not insist on being first.

Wait patiently for your turn.

Try not to be rude. Do not insist on having the best for yourself.

Try not to be rude. Do not insist on having the most for yourself.

Try not to be rude. Do not insist that everyone notice you and no one else.

Try not to be rude. Do not insist on having your own way all the time.

Avoid being rude by doing these things:

- Avoid saying anything that would hurt anyone.
- Avoid breaking or ruining anyone's things.
- Avoid talking while other people are talking.
- Avoid being noisy around people who need to have quiet.

It is important to treat other people the way you want to be treated.

If you do not want people to be rude to you, you must not be rude to them.

Joy Berry Enterprises
146 West 29th St., Suite 11RW
New York, NY 10001

Cover Design & Art Direction: John Bellaud
Cover Illustration & Art Production: Geoff Glisson

Printed in China
ISBN 978-1-60577-138-0